The ILLUSTRATED WORLD GUIDE to
ANIMALS

ANITA GANERI

THE INSIDE AND OUT GUIDE TO ANIMALS
was produced by

David West 👫 **Children's Books**
7 Princeton Court
55 Felsham Road
London SW15 1AZ

Designer: Rob Shone
Illustrators: Moorhen Studios
Editors: Dominique Crowley and Gail Bushnell
Picture Research: Victoria Cook
Consultant: Steve Parker

First published in Great Britain by Heinemann
Library, Halley Court, Jordan Hill, Oxford
OX2 8EJ, part of Harcourt Education.
Heinemann is a registered trademark
of Harcourt Education Ltd.

11 10 09 08 07
10 9 8 7 6 5 4 3 2 1

10 digit ISBN: 0 431 18304 X (hardback)
13 digit ISBN: 978 0 431 18304 6
10 digit ISBN: 0 431 18311 2 (paperback)
13 digit ISBN: 978 0 431 18311 4

Ganeri, Anita, 1961-
    Animals. - (The inside & out guides)
    1. Animals _ Juvenile literature
    I. Title
    590

Printed and bound in China

PHOTO CREDITS :
Abbreviations: t-top, m-middle, b-bottom, r-right,
l-left, c-centre.

Pages 4t, 17t, 19t, 24t, 25t, 27t Oxford Scientific;
15t, istockphoto.com.

Every effort has been made to contact copyright
holders of any material reproduced in this book.
Any omissions will be rectified in subsequent
printings if notice is given to the publishers.

*An explanation of difficult words can be
found in the glossary on pages 30 and 31.*

The INSIDE & OUT GUIDE to
ANIMALS

Anita Ganeri

Heinemann
LIBRARY

CONTENTS

5 INTRODUCTION

6 ZEBRA

8 DOLPHIN

10 KANGAROO

12 BIRD

14 CROCODILE

16 FROG

18 FISH

20 SHARK

22 GRASSHOPPER

24 SCORPION

26 LOBSTER

28 OCTOPUS

30 GLOSSARY

32 INDEX

INTRODUCTION

WELCOME TO THE WONDERFUL WORLD OF ANIMALS AND their amazing body features, inside and out. Many animals belonging to the same group share similar features and they are not simply for show. From long legs and razor-sharp teeth, to fins, wings and poisonous stings, these features allow animals to find food, escape from enemies and locate mates.

ZEBRA

ZEBRAS ARE MAMMALS – ANIMALS THAT ARE WARM-BLOODED, have backbones and feed their young on milk. They are members of a mammal family that also includes horses and donkeys. Zebras live on the African grasslands. Their bodies are designed for running over long distances, as they escape from predators and find grass to graze on.

ZEBRA HERD
Zebras are social animals and most live in herds several hundred animals strong. A single zebra is much more difficult for predators, such as lions, to catch if it is surrounded by other zebras.

MUSCLES

Most of a zebra's running power comes from its hind-quarters. It has large muscles in its rump which allow it to gallop at speeds of 70 km/h.

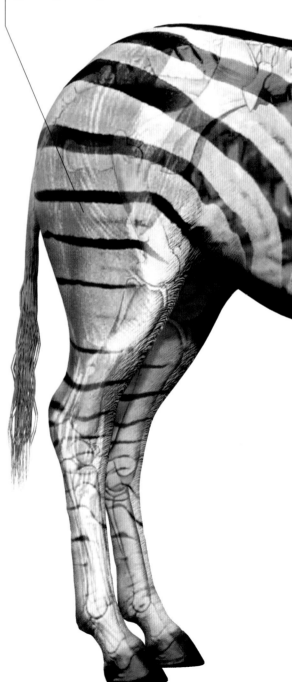

Like horses, zebras are medium-sized mammals with long heads and necks, and long legs for fast running. Each foot has one toe which is encased in a hoof. Zebras have manes running along the length of their necks, long tails and furry coats. Their long, sensitive ears can be swivelled around to pinpoint where sounds are coming from. To give good, all-round vision, zebras' eyes are set far back in their heads. They use their ears, noses and tails to show different moods. Zebras are **herbivores** and feed mainly on grass, although they will also eat bark, leaves and fruit. Their digestive system (see right) allows them to process large amounts of food very quickly.

The first horses lived in North America about 55 million years ago and were about the size of dogs. They had toes, rather than hooves, on their feet.

STRIPY COAT

A zebra's stripes look striking but they help to break up the zebra's outline when it is being chased by a predator. This makes it difficult to catch.

CHEST

A zebra has a deep chest with a large heart and lungs to help generate power for fast running.

Brain

TEETH

Zebras have sharp front **incisors** for cutting grass and broad cheek teeth for grinding.

Windpipe

Gullet

Heart

STOMACH

Zebras feed mainly on grass. The grass is digested in their stomachs, then passes into the next part of their gut where **bacteria** help to break it down.

RIDE 'EM!
Horses were first domesticated in Asia around 5,000 years ago. Since then, people have used horses for transport, in farming and for sport and leisure.

DOLPHIN

DOLPHINS ARE CETACEANS – MAMMALS WHICH HAVE adapted to life in the sea. They belong to the group of toothed whales which also includes orcas (killer whales). There are over 30 species of dolphins living in oceans around the world. Bottlenose dolphins are generally found in shallow water near the coast.

DOLPHIN POD

Some dolphins travel in groups called pods. The members of the pod seem to work together to round up shoals of fish to eat. In this way, they can catch far more fish than they could individually.

A dolphin is perfectly adapted for living in the water. Its body is streamlined and torpedo-shaped to cut smoothly through the water, propelled by a powerful tail. The dolphin's curved side-flippers are actually its forelimbs and are used for steering. Bottlenose dolphins have long, narrow jaws called 'beaks', filled with small, sharp teeth. The teeth are not used for chewing (dolphins swallow their **prey** whole) but for catching fish. To find their prey, dolphins use echo-location. They make a series of high-pitched clicks, which bounce off objects in the water. The returning echoes tell a dolphin where the objects are.

Kidneys

Muscle

SKIN

A dolphin's skin feels smooth and rubbery. It is extremely sensitive and is easily injured, but tends to heal quickly.

BOTTLENOSE DOLPHIN
TURSIOPS TRUNCATUS

A dolphin's nose is the blowhole on top of its head. It holds its breath as it dives. Then, when it surfaces, it blows out stale air in a smoke-like cloud of spray.

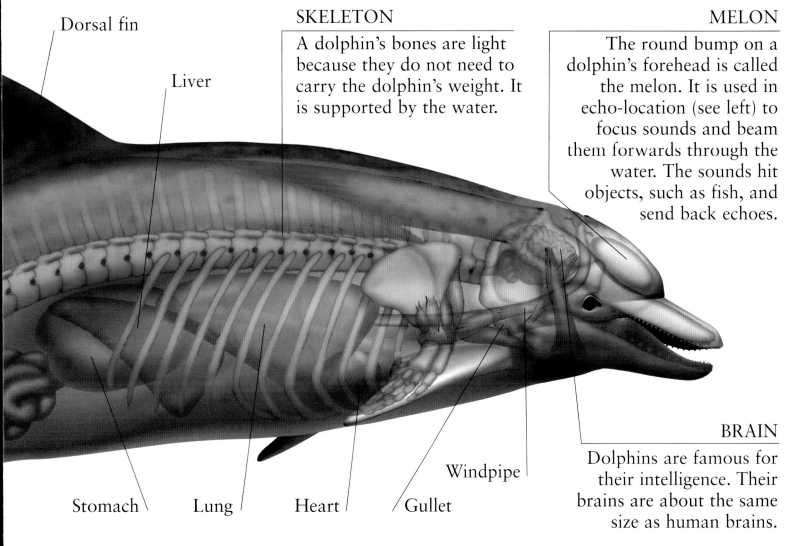

Dorsal fin

Liver

SKELETON

A dolphin's bones are light because they do not need to carry the dolphin's weight. It is supported by the water.

MELON

The round bump on a dolphin's forehead is called the melon. It is used in echo-location (see left) to focus sounds and beam them forwards through the water. The sounds hit objects, such as fish, and send back echoes.

BRAIN

Dolphins are famous for their intelligence. Their brains are about the same size as human brains.

Windpipe

Stomach   Lung   Heart   Gullet

FILTER FEEDERS
Baleen whales, like these humpbacks, do not have teeth. Instead, they have bony plates called baleen, hanging down from the roof of their mouths. The whales gulp in seawater and filter out food using the baleen plates as giant sieves.

9

KANGAROO

KANGAROOS ARE MARSUPIALS (MAMMALS WITH pouches). Other marsupials include koalas, wallabies and opossums. The majority of marsupials are found in Australia and New Guinea. Some species live in South America, and one in North America.

KANGAROO CARRIER

An older joey spends more time outside its mother's pouch, but is always ready to hop back in at the first sign of danger.

Weighing up to 90 kilograms and standing 165 centimetres tall, the red kangaroo is the largest of all the marsupials. With its short front limbs, long back limbs and long tail, the kangaroo is adapted for leaping across and grazing on the grassy plains where it lives. Kangaroos feed mainly on grasses and leaves. They get most of the water they need from plants and can survive for long periods without drinking. Unlike **placental mammals,** marsupials do not give birth to well-formed babies. A joey (baby kangaroo) is blind, weak and hairless. It manages to crawl from its mother's birth opening, through her fur, and up into her pouch where it attaches itself to a teat. It feeds on her milk and continues to grow for about seven months.

KOALA UP A GUM TREE
Koalas spend most of their lives in trees. Sharp claws on their paws allow them to grip and climb. Broad teeth in each jaw help them to grind up the eucalyptus leaves on which they feed.

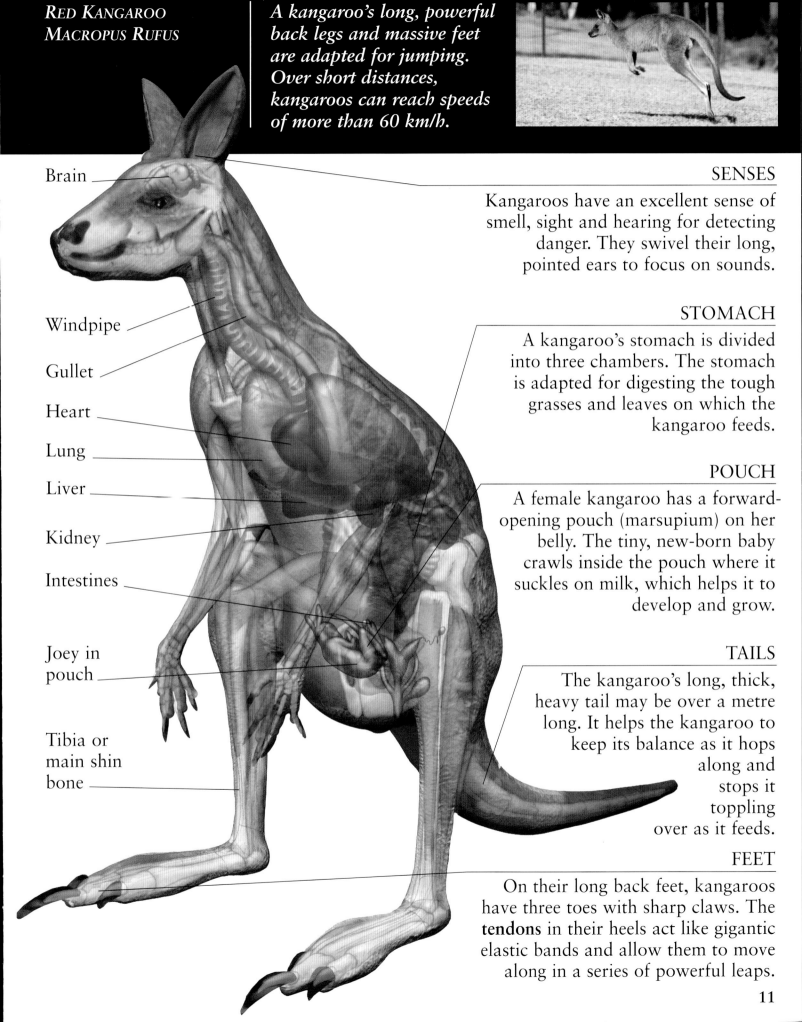

RED KANGAROO
MACROPUS RUFUS

A kangaroo's long, powerful back legs and massive feet are adapted for jumping. Over short distances, kangaroos can reach speeds of more than 60 km/h.

Brain

Windpipe

Gullet

Heart

Lung

Liver

Kidney

Intestines

Joey in pouch

Tibia or main shin bone

SENSES

Kangaroos have an excellent sense of smell, sight and hearing for detecting danger. They swivel their long, pointed ears to focus on sounds.

STOMACH

A kangaroo's stomach is divided into three chambers. The stomach is adapted for digesting the tough grasses and leaves on which the kangaroo feeds.

POUCH

A female kangaroo has a forward-opening pouch (marsupium) on her belly. The tiny, new-born baby crawls inside the pouch where it suckles on milk, which helps it to develop and grow.

TAILS

The kangaroo's long, thick, heavy tail may be over a metre long. It helps the kangaroo to keep its balance as it hops along and stops it toppling over as it feeds.

FEET

On their long back feet, kangaroos have three toes with sharp claws. The **tendons** in their heels act like gigantic elastic bands and allow them to move along in a series of powerful leaps.

11

BIRD

LIKE MAMMALS, BIRDS ARE WARM-BLOODED, AIR-BREATHING vertebrates. All birds have wings and feathers, although some are not able to fly. Flying birds share a similar body shape, perfectly adapted for life in the air. There are over 9,000 species of birds, living in habitats all over the world.

All birds share the same body plan, which is designed for flight. Their bodies are streamlined for cutting through the air, and their front limbs have become wings. To reduce weight, many of their larger bones are hollow. Birds have beaks instead of teeth, and feathers instead of fur or scales.

LUNGS

A bird's lungs are extremely good at taking oxygen from the air. Air is pulled through the lungs into air sacs, which reach right into the bird's wing bones. This system increases the flow of oxygen.

Stomach   Intestines   Kidneys

Brain

Ear

Windpipe

CROP

A bird stores swallowed food in its bag-like crop. The food then passes into its muscular **gizzard** to be ground up.

Heart

TENDONS

When a bird lands on a branch, its weight makes its leg tendons tighten to clamp its toes firmly to its perch.

Liver

Keel (breastbone)

MUSCLES

The power needed for flight is provided by two sets of massive muscles fixed to the bird's large breastbone. They flap the wings up and down.

Each year, many birds make long flights, called migrations. They fly from their summer breeding grounds to warmer climates where food is more plentiful.

Tail feathers

MOTHER GOOSE
All birds lay hard-shelled eggs. Most build nests to provide a safe place to lay their eggs and raise their young.

FLIGHT FEATHERS
Long, strong feathers on the bird's wings form the curved shape that provides lift. They can also be used for steering in the air.

SKELETON
Many of the bones in a flying bird's skeleton are hollow, with air spaces inside. In many flightless birds, the bones are solid and heavier.

FLAPPING FLIGHT
All birds flap their wings to gain height and speed as they fly. Flapping produces thrust to push the bird along on both the up and down strokes. The push of the downstroke, together with the shape of the bird's wing, also produces lift.

downstroke

upstroke

CROCODILE

Crocodiles and their relatives, the alligators and gharials, share a similar body plan. They have armour-plated bodies, long tails, short limbs and long-snouted heads. Their bodies

are adapted for life in the water where they hunt their prey. Crocodiles are **carnivores**, feeding on fish, birds and mammals. They use their sharp, pointed teeth for grabbing prey, which they tear apart by shaking their heads. Crocodiles hunt by lying almost submerged in the water until their prey comes close enough for them to strike.

CROCODILE CRECHE

Crocodiles are caring mothers. The female digs a nest and lays her eggs in it. She sits near the nest for about three months, until the eggs hatch. Then she carries her babies to the water.

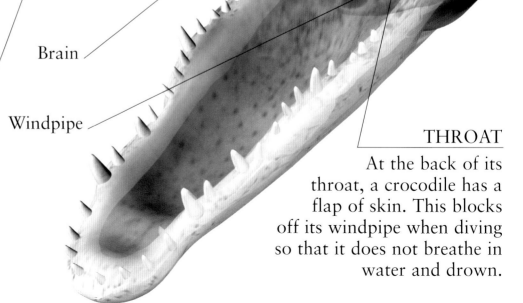

NOSTRILS

A crocodile's nostrils are on top of its head so that it can breathe when it is floating, half submerged, in the water. Crocodiles have a very sharp sense of smell which they use to track down prey and mates, and detect danger.

Brain

Windpipe

THROAT

At the back of its throat, a crocodile has a flap of skin. This blocks off its windpipe when diving so that it does not breathe in water and drown.

Crocodiles have an extra eyelid which closes when they are diving to protect their eyes. The eyelid is see-through so that the crocodile can still see clearly.

SKIN

A crocodile's protective armour is made from rough, horny plates, called scutes, running along its back and tail.

TAIL

A crocodile moves its broad, muscular tail from side to side to push its body through the water. It also uses its tail to accelerate very quickly and to change direction.

Kidneys

ANKLES

On land, crocodiles usually walk along with their feet and legs splayed out to the sides. They can also twist their ankles around to raise their bodies and tails off the ground.

Liver

Lungs

Heart

STOMACH

A crocodile's stomach stretches to hold large pieces of prey. Some crocodiles swallow stones and rocks to help them grind up hard shells and bones, and to stabilise their bodies in the water.

REPTILE RELATIVES
The three main groups of reptiles are crocodiles, turtles, and lizards and snakes. They all share certain physical features, such as scaly skin, even though their bodies are very different shapes.

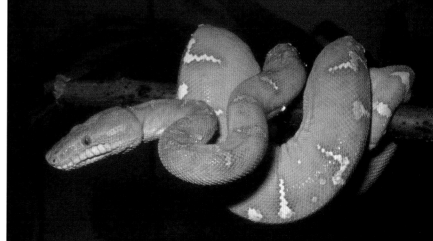

FROG

FROGS ARE AMPHIBIANS, A WORD WHICH MEANS 'HAVING TWO lives'. These animals spend part of their lives in water and part of their lives on land. Other types of amphibians include toads, salamanders, newts and caecilians. Like crocodiles and other reptiles, and also fish, amphibians are cold-blooded vertebrates.

TREE FROG
Many tree frogs have loose skin on their bellies and sticky webbing between their toes to help them cling to tree trunks.

All species of frog share the same body plan, with short, squat bodies, long back legs and smooth, slimy skin. Combined with their lack of tails, these features are all connected to the frog's jumping way of life on land. Frogs leap to escape from enemies and sometimes to catch their prey. Frogs are also adapted to life in the water, where they return to mate and lay their eggs (see right). Their eyes and nostrils are on top of their heads so that they can see and breathe while the rest of their body is hidden underwater. Their back legs have webbed toes for pushing against the water as they swim.

EAR
Most species of frogs have large eardrums on either side of their heads, just behind their eyes. A good sense of hearing is important for listening out for mating calls (see right).

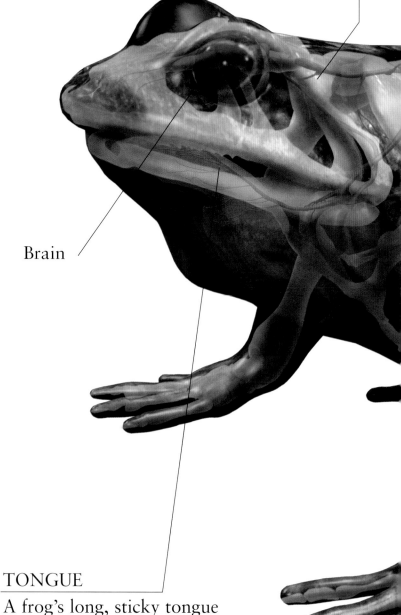

Brain

TONGUE
A frog's long, sticky tongue can be flicked out quickly to catch insects. The frog curls its tongue back to reel in its prey.

Many male frogs croak, click or call to attract females for mating. As they call, they blow up their vocal sacs with air. This helps to produce a sound.

LUNGS AND SKIN

Frogs have sac-like lungs for breathing oxygen from the air. A frog can also take in oxygen directly through its moist skin. As tadpoles, frogs use their gills to take in oxygen dissolved in the water.

Kidneys

BACKBONE

Frogs have only six to ten vertebrae in their spines. This gives them short, stiff backbones which help their bodies cope with the forces involved in leaping and landing.

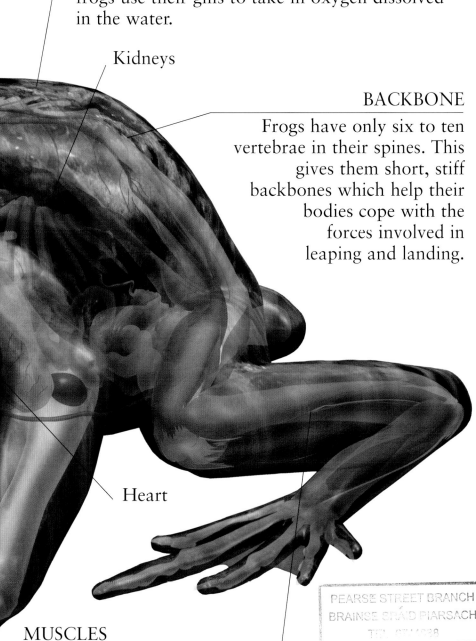

Heart

MUSCLES

A frog has long back legs with powerful muscles that launch it into the air as it hops or leaps. They are also useful for swimming.

FROG LIFE-CYCLE

A frog starts life as an egg (1), laid in water. It grows (2) before hatching into a tadpole (3). It develops a tail, along with gills (4). Gradually, the tadpole's tail shrinks (5). It grows legs and lungs, and turns into a tiny frog (6) that can live on land.

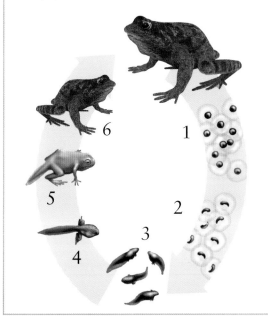

SALAMANDER

Salamanders have longer bodies than frogs, shorter legs and long tails. Some brightly-coloured species have poisonous skins.

FISH

LIKE REPTILES AND AMPHIBIANS, FISH ARE COLD-BLOODED vertebrates. They live in oceans, rivers and lakes all over the world. The two main types of fish are bony fish (like the rockfish shown below) and cartilaginous fish (shown on pages 20–21).

STICKING TOGETHER

Some small fish live in huge shoals. This gives safety in numbers, making it difficult for predators to pick out individual fish from among the crowd.

Most bony fish, such as this rockfish, have muscular, streamlined bodies, which are ideally suited to their watery way of life. A powerful tail and flexible backbone allow the fish to swim by making a series of S-shaped curves. Side and back fins help the fish to balance and steer. For 'breathing' underwater, fish have gills instead of the lungs of land animals. They gulp in mouthfuls of water which wash over their gills. In the gills, oxygen from the water passes into the fish's blood to be carried around its body. The gills are fine and feathery, giving a large surface area to take in the maximum amount of oxygen possible.

GILLS

Fish have feathery gills on each side of their heads for breathing. The gills take in oxygen dissolved in the water. A hard flap protects the gills of **bony fish**.

Brain

Heart

Liver

Pelvic fin

NOSTRILS

Fish have one or two pairs of nostrils. These open into chambers lined with sensors which detect smell chemicals in the water. Fish use smell to detect food and danger.

Lungfish are unusual because they have lungs as well as gills. This allows them to breathe at the surface in times of drought.

Dorsal fin

LATERAL LINE

The lateral line is a fluid-filled tube that runs along each side of a fish's body. It picks up underwater vibrations caused by currents and other creatures.

FINS

These flexible, wing-like structures help fish to balance in water and aid steering when swimming. They are moved by muscles within a fish's body.

Caudal fin

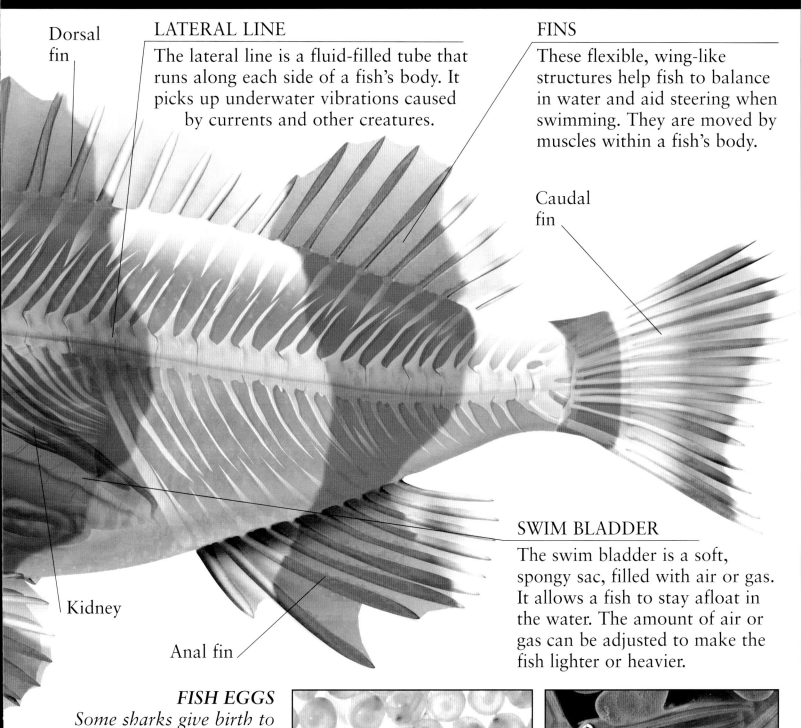

Kidney

Anal fin

SWIM BLADDER

The swim bladder is a soft, spongy sac, filled with air or gas. It allows a fish to stay afloat in the water. The amount of air or gas can be adjusted to make the fish lighter or heavier.

FISH EGGS

Some sharks give birth to live young but most fish lay eggs in the water. Some fish, such as cod, lay millions of tiny eggs, in the hope that some will survive.

SHARK

SHARKS BELONG TO THE GROUP OF CARTILAGINOUS FISH, which also includes rays, skates and chimera. Instead of bone, these fish have skeletons made of cartilage, a tough, gristle-like material. This makes the skeleton very strong, flexible and light.

Although sharks come in different shapes and sizes, the sleek, streamlined body of the great white shark is the most famous of all. The great white is built for hunting at speed. It detects its prey with finely-tuned senses, then charges and bites with bone-crushing force. Its jaws are lined with razor-sharp teeth, which are constantly being replaced. As the shark bites, an extra eyelid closes across the eyes to protect them. If prey is too large to eat in one gulp, the shark shakes its head from side to side until it has sawn off a manageable chunk of flesh.

MANEATERS
Many sharks have a reputation as maneaters. But only a few species have been known to kill people. They include the great white and hammerhead (above).

RAY
Closely related to sharks, rays have very large side fins which give their bodies a diamond shape. Most rays hide on the sea bed, lying in wait for their prey of fish, crabs, shrimps, sand eels and worms.

GREAT WHITE SHARK CARCHARODON CARCHARIAS

Weighing in at 20 tonnes, the whale shark is the largest fish. This giant feeds on tiny animals which it strains from the water through sieve-like gills.

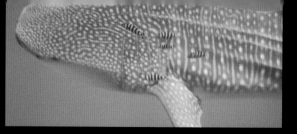

GUTS

A shark's guts are quite short but they are not a simple tube. A screw-shaped 'spiral valve' inside gives a larger surface area for absorbing digested food.

LIVER

Sharks do not have swim bladders. Their large livers are filled with oil, which is lighter than water. This, and a light skeleton, may help sharks' ability to float.

SENSORY SYSTEM

Sharp senses of sight and smell help sharks to find their prey. Special organs in their snouts can detect electrical signals given off by prey's muscles.

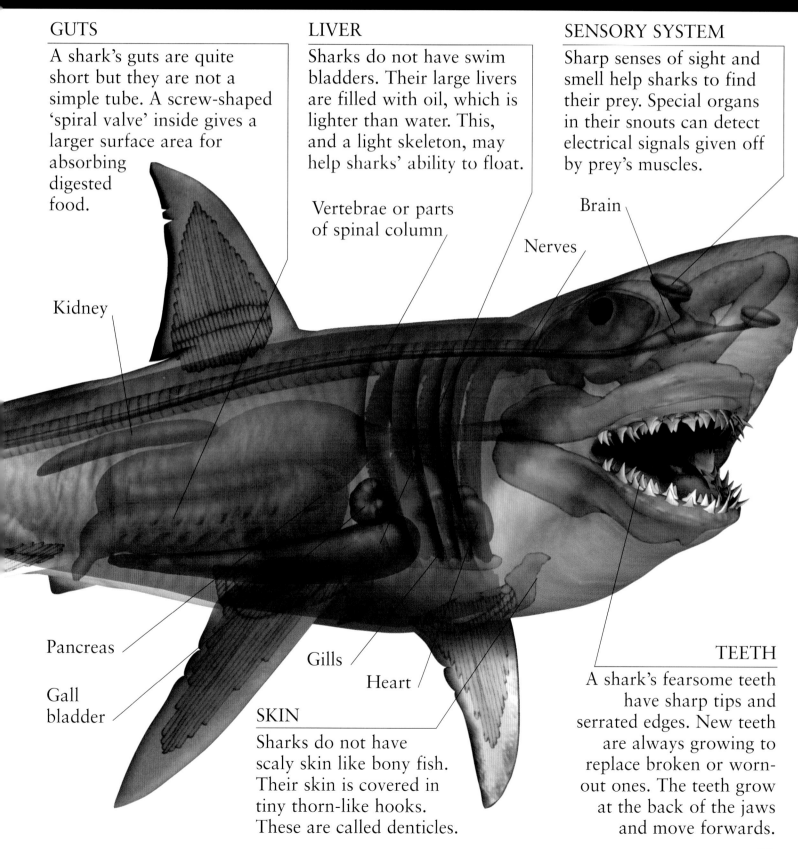

Kidney

Vertebrae or parts of spinal column

Nerves

Brain

Pancreas

Gall bladder

Gills

Heart

SKIN

Sharks do not have scaly skin like bony fish. Their skin is covered in tiny thorn-like hooks. These are called denticles.

TEETH

A shark's fearsome teeth have sharp tips and serrated edges. New teeth are always growing to replace broken or worn-out ones. The teeth grow at the back of the jaws and move forwards.

GRASSHOPPER

GRASSHOPPERS BELONG TO THE largest group of animals on Earth, called the arthropods. Like all arthropods, they have legs that bend at joints and bodies divided into sections. Other arthropods include spiders, shrimps, centipedes, and millipedes.

Grasshoppers are insects, the largest group of arthropods. They have typical three-part insect bodies (the head, thorax and abdomen), two pairs of wings and six legs. Their long back legs are adapted for jumping (see right). Male grasshoppers have special features on their bodies to help them produce chirping songs. They use these to attract a mate, using a technique called stridulation. Short-horned grasshoppers, like this one, scrape their back legs against their front wings. Long-horned grasshoppers rub their front wings together. A grasshopper picks up the sounds with its 'ears'. These are thin, film-like membranes in its abdomen, attached to sound sensors. Sounds cause the membranes to vibrate and this triggers the sensors.

LOCUST EATERS
Locusts are grasshoppers that form gigantic swarms and strip farmers' fields of their crops.

Antenna

Eye

Head

Thorax

Foot

Footpad

SALIVARY GLANDS

A grasshopper's mouthparts are designed for chewing on plants. Glands in the grasshopper's mouth pour watery saliva on to the food to break it down.

HEART

A grasshopper's heart is part of a tube in its abdomen. It pumps blood along the rest of the tube to the head. Then the blood seeps around the grasshopper's body.

GRASSHOPPER
CHORTHIPPUS BRUNNEUS

Katydids are grasshoppers skilled in camouflage. Many have bodies that look like leaves (living and dead) or lichen to hide from their enemies.

GUT

There are three parts to a grasshopper's gut. Food is swallowed and passes into a bag-like crop for storage. Next, it passes into the midgut where it is digested. Waste collects in the hindgut until it is passed out through the end of the abdomen.

Malpighian tubules or waste organ

LIFE UNDERGROUND

During the day mole crickets use their strong forelegs to burrow through damp sand and soil. They feed on plants and any small insects that they can catch.

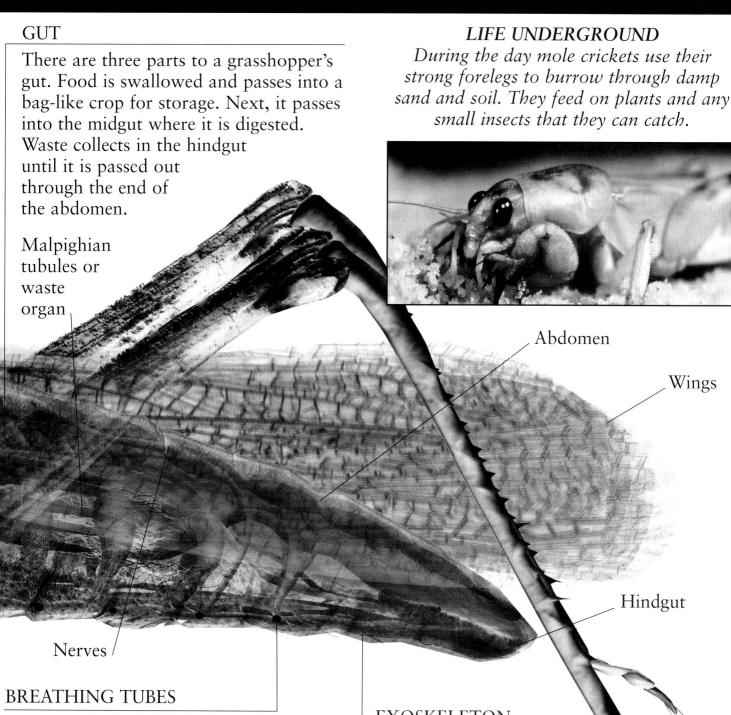

Abdomen

Wings

Nerves

Hindgut

BREATHING TUBES

Air passes into the grasshopper's body through holes called spiracles in its **exoskeleton**. The air travels down tiny tubes called tracheae and around the grasshopper's body. Waste carbon dioxide passes out of the spiracles.

EXOSKELETON

Grasshoppers do not have a bony skeleton inside their bodies. Instead, they have a tough body casing called the exoskeleton. It protects the grasshopper's soft inner parts.

SCORPION

LIKE INSECTS, SCORPIONS ARE ARTHROPODS. They belong to a group of arthropods called arachnids, which also includes spiders, ticks and mites. At first sight, they may not look alike but all arachnids share a similar body plan.

Scorpions and their arachnid relations have bodies divided into two parts. These are called the cephalothorax (head and thorax) and the abdomen. Four pairs of legs are attached to the cephalothorax. There is also a pair of large pincers called pedipalps. These are used for grabbing prey, scaring off enemies and in courtship (see right). The back end of the scorpion's abdomen narrows to form a distinctive arched 'tail' with a sting at the end. Scorpions spend the day hiding under rocks or logs, coming out at night to hunt for prey. They feed on beetles, cockroaches and other small animals. Having sensed their prey (see right), they sit and wait for it to move within range. Then they grab it in their massive pincers. When hunting scorpions use their poisonous stings if their prey is very large. Mainly, their stings are used in self defence.

BABIES ON BOARD
A female scorpion carries her babies on her back for a few days until they are big enough to look after themselves.

EIGHT-LEGGED SPINNER
Spiders are famous for producing silk. Some use silk to spin sticky webs in which to trap their prey. Others, like this wolf spider, hunt on the ground but line their burrows with silk.

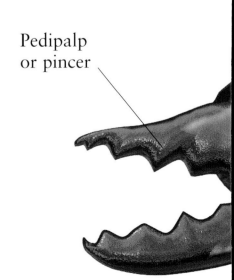

Pedipalp or pincer

Before mating, a male and female scorpion hold each other's pincers and 'dance'. After mating, the female lays her eggs which hatch very quickly.

HEART

Scorpions and other arachnids have tube-shaped hearts, which pump blood around their bodies. Their blood is colourless and, in some species, is poisonous.

POISON GLAND

The sting at the tip of a scorpion's tail is called the telson. It is supplied with poison by a bag-like poison gland. Some scorpion poison is strong enough to kill a human being.

Chelicerae or mouthparts

Median eyes

Coxal gland or waste organ

Exoskeleton

Digestive glands

Stomach

Malpighian tubules or waste organ

BOOK LUNGS

Scorpions breathe through special organs called book lungs. These have many flaps, a bit like the pages of a book. The flaps give a large surface area for taking in oxygen.

Salivary gland

Brain

PECTINES

Under its abdomen, a scorpion has a pair of comb-like pectines. These brush against the ground and detect vibrations, which help the scorpion to sense and locate its prey.

25

LOBSTER

TOGETHER WITH CRABS, KRILL AND BARNACLES, lobsters are crustaceans. All of these animals have soft bodies protected by hard shells. Most crustaceans live in the ocean or in fresh water. Only a few, including woodlice and some crabs, have adapted to life on the land.

Like scorpions, lobsters are arthropods. They have bodies divided into segments, and legs that bend at joints. Lobsters have ten pairs of legs. The first two legs are its huge claws. The larger claw is called the crusher claw, used to squash the shells of the lobster's prey. The smaller claw is the pincer claw, used for cutting the soft flesh. The other legs are mostly used for walking and grooming. The lobster's hard outer casing or shell is its exoskeleton, which helps to protect its soft body.

Abdomen

GILLS

A lobster's gills are washed with water which passes through openings between the lobster's legs.

HEART

A lobster's heart has a single chamber and several openings. It beats between 50–100 times per minute to pump blue blood around the lobster's body.

CRAB COUSIN

Like lobsters, crabs have hard shells around their bodies. These cannot stretch as the crabs grow, so they are moulted. As the crab breaks out of its old shell, its body grows quickly before its new exoskeleton hardens.

COMMON LOBSTER
HOMARUS GAMMARUS

Each year, thousands of spiny lobsters migrate along the Atlantic coast. They march in single file, hooking their claws on to the lobster in front.

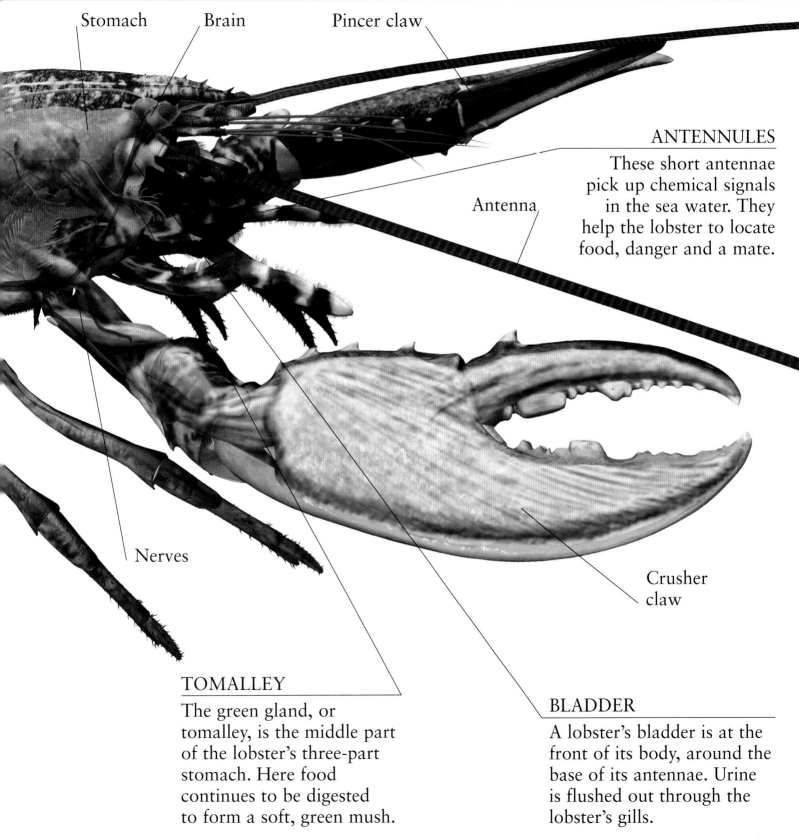

Stomach

Brain

Pincer claw

ANTENNULES

These short antennae pick up chemical signals in the sea water. They help the lobster to locate food, danger and a mate.

Antenna

Nerves

Crusher claw

TOMALLEY

The green gland, or tomalley, is the middle part of the lobster's three-part stomach. Here food continues to be digested to form a soft, green mush.

BLADDER

A lobster's bladder is at the front of its body, around the base of its antennae. Urine is flushed out through the lobster's gills.

OCTOPUS

THESE MOLLUSCS ARE RELATED TO SQUID, SLUGS, snails, oysters and clams. Unlike their crusty cousins, though, the only hard part of an octopus is its beak, which resembles the beak of a parrot. Octopuses have a short life. Some species die after just six months, while larger ones might live for up to five years.

With eight long arms equipped with suckers, octopuses are easy to recognise. Because they do not have shells, they can squeeze their rubbery bodies into cracks in the sea bed rocks where they hide from predators, or lie in wait for their prey to pass by. They use their arms to catch prey and to crawl about on the sea floor. Octopuses have several ways of escaping from enemies. They may use ink to confuse predators (see right), or suck in water then shoot it out again to propel their bodies backwards. Octopuses can also change colour by opening and closing colour cells in their skin. They use this clever trick to camouflage themselves, show their different moods and send signals to other octopuses.

NERVOUS SYSTEM

Octopuses have amazingly sophisticated nervous systems with large brains and eyes. They have good memories and are among the most intelligent of all the **invertebrates**.

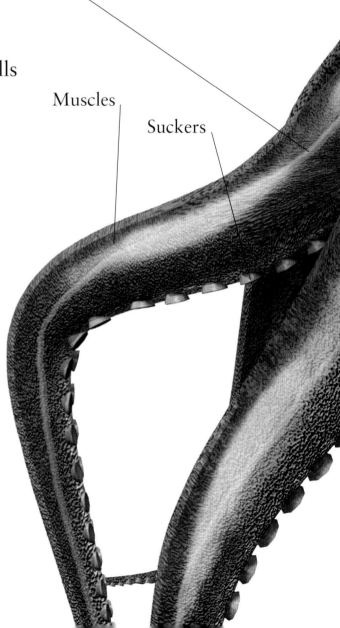

Muscles

Suckers

SUCKERS
Octopus tentacles are armed with circular suckers, each controlled by tiny muscles. They are used for grasping prey and feeling. They are very sensitive and detect textures, patterns and tastes.

COMMON OCTOPUS
OCTOPUS VULGARIS

As well as changing colour some octopuses can also change their skin texture. This helps them to hide among craggy rocks and seaweed.

Brain Poison gland Salivary glands Crop

Stomach

BEAK

An octopus uses its hard, parrot-like beak for killing and tearing prey. Many octopuses have poisonous bites.

INK SAC

To escape from predators, an octopus squirts out a cloud of thick black ink from a special ink sac.

Kidney

HEARTS

An octopus has three hearts (two are shown here). The main heart pumps blood through its body while two others pump blood through its gills. Octopus blood is blue because it contains copper for carrying oxygen.

Gills

Siphon or breathing tube

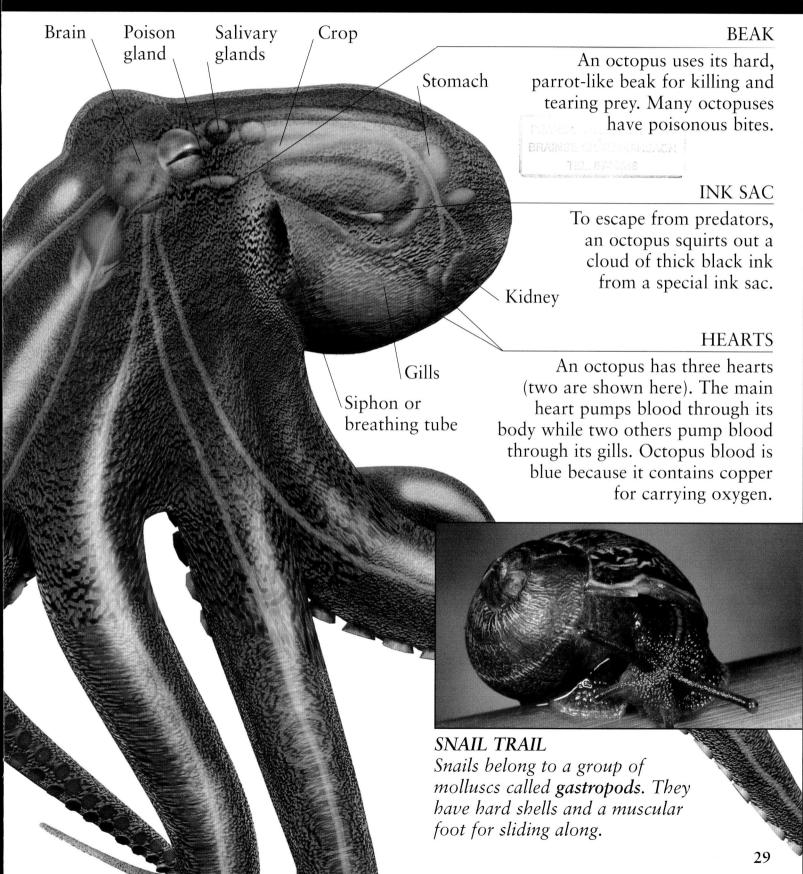

SNAIL TRAIL
*Snails belong to a group of molluscs called **gastropods**. They have hard shells and a muscular foot for sliding along.*

29

GLOSSARY

amphibians
Cold-blooded vertebrates, such as frogs and toads, that spend part of their lives in water and part on land.

arachnids
Invertebrates, such as spiders and scorpions, that have two parts to their bodies and four pairs of legs.

arthropods
The largest group of invertebrates, it includes insects, arachnids, crustaceans, and centipedes.

bacteria
Tiny living things that are found almost everywhere.

bony fish
Fish that have skeletons made from bone as opposed to cartilage.

caecilians
Amphibians that have long bodies, no tails and live buried in damp soil.

carnivores
Animals that feed on meat.

cartilaginous fish
Fish that have skeletons made from gristly cartilage, instead of bone.

cetaceans
The group of mammals that have adapted to life in the sea, including dolphins and whales.

chimeras
A group of cartilaginous fish related to sharks. They are also called ratfish or rabbit fish.

cold-blooded
Animals, such as fish, reptiles and amphibians that cannot control their own body temperature. They rely on the external temperature to warm them up or cool them down.

crop
A pouch-like part of an animal's digestive system where food is stored for digestion.

crustaceans
The group of arthropods which includes crabs, lobsters, and woodlice. They have segmented bodies and jointed legs.

exoskeleton
The tough, outer coat or shell of invertebrates that protects and supports their soft bodies.

gastropods
The group of molluscs that includes snails and slugs.

gizzard
A bird's second stomach, which is used for grinding up its food.

herbivores
Animals that eat plants.

incisors
Sharp, front teeth for cutting food.

invertebrates
Animals that do not have backbones or skeletons inside their bodies.

mammals
Warm-blooded vertebrates that breathe air using lungs and feed their young on milk.

marsupials
A group of mammals that have pouches where their young feed on milk and grow.

migrations
Long journeys made by many animals, especially birds, between their breeding and feeding grounds.

molluscs
The group of invertebrates that includes squid, octopuses, snails, clams, and mussels. Molluscs have soft bodies, often protected by hard shells.

placental mammals
Mammals whose young grow inside their mothers' bodies until they are well formed.

predators
Animals that hunt other animals for food.

prey
Animals that are hunted and eaten by other animals.

reptiles
Cold-blooded vertebrates, with scaly skin, most of which lay rubbery-shelled eggs. Reptiles include snakes, lizards, crocodiles and turtles.

tendons
Strong, flexible bands that attach muscles to bones.

vertebrates
Animals with backbones and skeletons inside their bodies.

warm-blooded
Animals that can control their own body temperature to stay the same whatever the conditions outside.

INDEX

amphibians
  frogs 16, 17
  salamanders 17
arachnids
  scorpions 24, 25
  spiders 24

birds 12, 13
  geese 13
  magpies 12, 13
bony fish 18, 19

carnivores 14
cartilaginous fish 20, 21
cetaceans 8
crabs 26
crocodiles 14, 15
crustaceans
  crabs 26
  lobsters 26, 27

dolphins 8, 9

echo-location 8, 9

fish
  bays 20
  bony 18, 19
  cartilaginous 20, 21
  flag rockfish 18,19
  lungfish 19

fish(continued)
  sharks 20, 21
flag rockfish 18, 19
flying 12, 13
frogs 16, 17

gastropods 29
geese 13
grasshoppers 22, 23

herbivores 6
horses 7

insects
  grasshoppers 22, 23
  katydids 23

kangaroos 10, 11
katydids 23

lobsters 26, 27
lungfish 19

magpies 12, 13
mammals
  dolphins 8, 9
  horses 7
  kangaroos 10, 11
  koalas 10
  whales 8, 9
  zebras 6, 7

marsupials 10, 11
  kangaroos 10, 11
  koalas 10
migration 13
molluscs
  octopuses 28, 29
  snails 29

octopuses 28, 29

rays 20
reptiles
  crocodiles 14, 15
  snakes 15

salamanders 17
scorpions 24, 25
sharks 20, 21
snails 29
snakes 15
spiders 24

whales 8,9

zebras 6,7